The Happiest Day

by Ruth Shannon Odor
illustrated by Helen Endres

THE CHILD'S WORLD

ELGIN, ILLINOIS 60120

Library of Congress Cataloging in Publication Data

Odor, Ruth Shannon.
  The happiest day.

  (Bible story books)
  SUMMARY: Retells the story of Christ's resurrection
and how he revealed himself to his friends.
  1. Jesus Christ—Resurrection—Juvenile literature.
[1. Jesus Christ—Resurrection.   2. Bible stories—
N.T.]   I. Endres, Helen.   II. Title.   III. Series.
BT481.037   232.9'7   79-12184
ISBN 0-89565-085-1

Distributed by Standard Publishing, 8121 Hamilton Avenue,
Cincinnati, Ohio 45231.

The Happiest Day

The Biblical account of this story
is in *Matthew 28:1-10; Mark 16:1-8, 14;*
and *Luke 24:1-10, 36-49.*

It was a sad day—at the beginning—
    that Sunday long ago.
It was a sad, sad day
    for Jesus' friends.

It was dark, for the sun had not yet risen.
Some women walked along the road
in the darkness.
Big tears rolled down their cheeks.

Jesus, their best friend, was gone.
Jesus was dead.
Two days earlier, he had died,
on a cross.
People had laid His body in a tomb.
People had rolled a big stone
in front of the door.

The women knew.
They had been there.

The bright sun peeped up over the hills.
It was a beautiful day,
   that Sunday long ago.
But the women didn't notice.

"Oh, we forgot something," said Salome.
"Who will roll the big stone away?
It is too heavy for us."

"We should have thought of that," said Mary.

"What shall we do?" asked Joanna.

"Look!" said Salome. "The stone has already been rolled away."

"The door of the tomb is open!" said Mary.

"How can that be?" asked Joanna.

"I must go and tell the others!" said Mary Magdalene.

And she ran as fast as she could go.

The women peeped inside.
The body of Jesus was not there!
The tomb was empty…except…
   except for two angels,
   two angels bright as lightning,
   dressed in clothes as white as snow!

"Don't be afraid," said one
of the angels.
"I know you are looking for Jesus.
He is not here. He has risen.
Go tell the rest of His friends.
Tell them Jesus is alive."

The women still didn't understand.
This wonderful news—
    how could it be true?
They ran.
They ran as fast as they could.

As the women hurried along the road,
     suddenly Jesus met them!
It was Jesus! Jesus Himself!
He was alive!
The angel's words were true!
The women knelt before Jesus.
How happy they were!

"Don't be afraid," Jesus said.
"Go and tell my friends.
Soon they will see Me."

And that is just what the women did.

"Jesus is alive!" the women said.
"He has risen from the dead!
We have seen Him!"

"We can hardly believe it,"
        said Jesus' friends.
"It is too good to be true."

But later that day, they knew it was true.
For they, too, saw Jesus!
Suddenly He was in the room
    where they were.

"Why are you troubled?"
asked Jesus.
"It is really I.
I told you I would rise
from the dead."

How happy Jesus' friends were!
Jesus was alive!
He had risen from the dead!

It was a happy day,
    that Sunday long ago.
It was the happiest day
    Jesus' friends had ever known!

And all through the years,
and still today,
Jesus' friends are happy.

For Jesus is risen
from the dead.